50 cross stitch QUICKIES
Animals & Friends

Show your fondness for the animal world with this big assortment of miniature cross stitch designs from Plaid's® Bucilla® Needlecrafts. With stitch counts of 35 by 35 or less each, the designs are perfect for little gifts and accessories.

Animals of the Sky

Let your imagination take flight with creative plans for these designs of birds, butterflies, a bee, a ladybug, and a dragonfly. The tiny hummingbird is sure to make hearts flutter.

LEISURE ARTS, INC. • Maumelle, Arkansas

Hummingbird

Stitch Count: 30w x 21h

Design Size: 2¼" x 1½" on 14 count white Aida

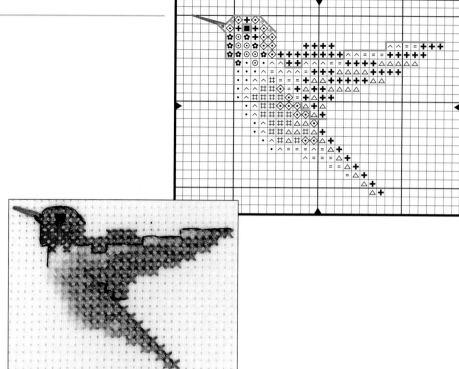

Cross Stitch-2 strands

⊙	350	coral
✿	349	dk coral
⊞	470	green
◈	469	dk green
^	644	beige grey
=	642	dk beige grey
△	646	grey
✛	645	dk grey
■	310	black
·	blanc	white

Backstitch-1 strand

╱	310	black

Straight Stitch-2 strands

╱	645	dk grey

Bee

Stitch Count: 31w x 31h

Design Size: 2¼" x 2¼" on 14 count white Aida

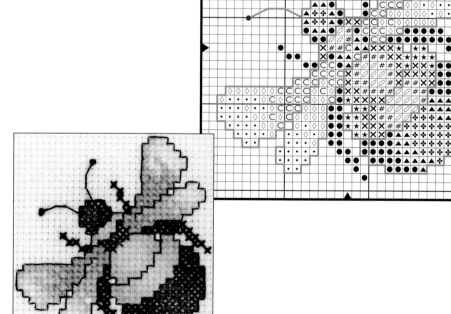

Cross Stitch-2 strands

∅	745	vy lt yellow
#	744	lt yellow
✕	743	yellow
★	742	dk yellow
◇	415	lt grey
C	318	grey
✤	413	dk grey
▲	3799	charcoal
●	310	black
·	blanc	white

Backstitch-1 strand

╱	310	black

French Knot-2 strands

●	310	black

Goldfinch

Stitch Count: 33w x 27h

Design Size: 2⅜" x 2" on 14 count white Aida

Cross Stitch-2 strands

○	744	yellow
Y	743	yellow-orange
☆	742	dk yellow-orange
✳	3854	lt apricot
✖	435	lt brown
▼	413	dk grey
■	310	black
·	blanc	white

Backstitch-1 strand

╱	310	black

Ladybug

Stitch Count: 27w x 33h

Design Size: 2" x 2⅜" on 14 count white Aida

Cross Stitch-2 strands

╱	3708	lt melon
△	3706	melon
♡	3801	dk melon
˙·.	666	bright red
⊠	321	lt red
T	304	dk red
■	498	vy dk red
=	317	dk grey
m	413	vy dk grey
✖	3799	charcoal
◆	310	black
O	blanc	white

Backstitch-1 strand

╱	310	black

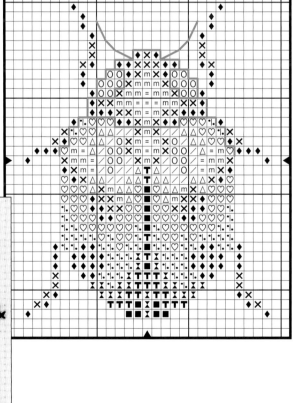

Cardinal

Stitch Count: 33w x 32h

Design Size: 2⅜" x 2⅜" on 14 count white Aida

Cross Stitch-2 strands

⊞	351	lt coral
♡	350	coral
⊙	349	dk coral
✿	817	vy dk coral
Y	3854	lt apricot
✳	3853	apricot
◈	469	green
◆	433	brown
■	310	black

Backstitch-1 strand

╱	310	black

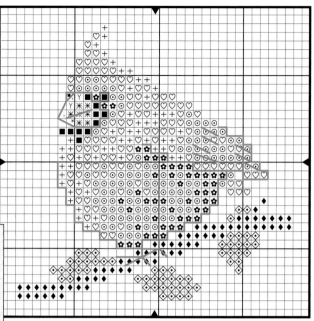

Robin

Stitch Count: 29w x 32h

Design Size: 2⅛" x 2⅜" on 14 count white Aida

Cross Stitch-2 strands

◇	761	lt dusty rose
H	760	dusty rose
Y	3853	apricot
✳	921	terra cotta
✿	920	dk terra cotta
◆	433	brown
⊠	318	lt grey
⊡	414	grey
▼	413	dk grey
■	310	black

Backstitch-1 strand

╱	310	black

Backstitch-2 strands

╱	433	brown
╱	blanc	white

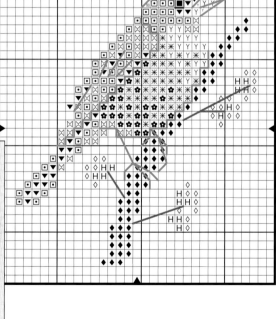

Dragonfly

Stitch Count: 34w x 34h

Design Size: 2½" x 2½" on 14 count white Aida

Cross Stitch-2 strands

╱	772	pale green
A	3348	lt green
♣	3347	green
♡	996	bright blue
#	3843	dk bright blue
♦	995	vy dk bright blue
☆	762	vy lt grey
O	blanc	white

Backstitch-1 strand

╱	413	dk grey
╱	310	black

French Knot-2 strands

●	310	black

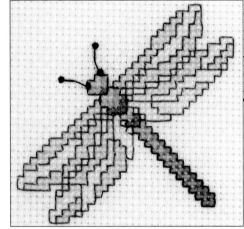

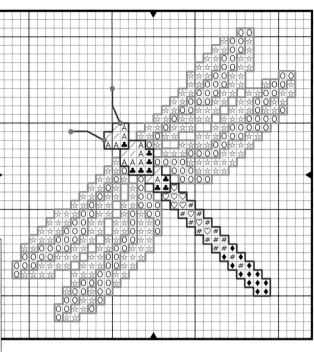

Monarch Butterfly

Stitch Count: 31w x 23h

Design Size: 2¼" x 1¾" on 14 count white Aida

Cross Stitch-2 strands

Y	743	lt yellow orange
☆	742	yellow orange
◇	970	tangerine
+	947	dk tangerine
△	946	vy dk tangerine
▼	413	dk grey
■	310	black
·	blanc	white

Backstitch-1 strand

╱	310	black

French Knot-2 strands

◔	742	yellow orange
●	310	black
⬤	blanc	white

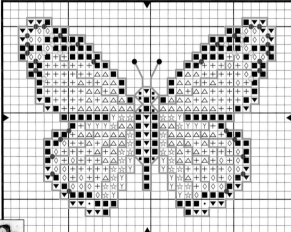

Blue Butterfly

Stitch Count: 35w x 24h

Design Size: 2½" x 1¾" on 14 count white Aida

Cross Stitch-2 strands

⟋	747	pale turquoise
+	3811	vy lt turquoise
♡	598	lt turquoise
⬝⊦	597	turquoise
→	3810	dk turquoise
⟂	3809	vy dk turquoise
=	414	lt grey
C	317	grey
✕	413	dk grey
◆	3799	charcoal
●	310	black
▢	blanc	white

Backstitch-1 strand

⟋	310	black

French Knot-2 strands

●	310	black

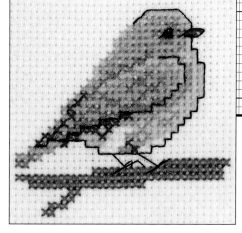

Bluebird

Stitch Count: 33w x 30h

Design Size: 2⅜" x 2¼" on 14 count white Aida

Cross Stitch-2 strands

⌃	353	lt coral
C	352	coral
=	827	lt blue
⊞	813	blue
+	826	dk blue
✕	435	lt brown
▼	413	dk grey
■	310	black
•	blanc	white

Backstitch-1 strand

⟋	310	black

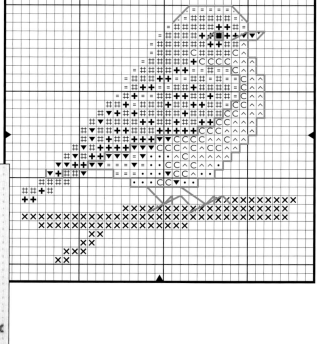

Farm Animals

Cultivate a feeling of country charm with a menagerie of farm animals. This collection rounds up a pony, cow, pig, goat, sheep, bunny, and chickens. And, of course, no farm is complete without the family cat and dog.

Pony

Stitch Count: 35w x 35h

Design Size: 2½" x 2½" on 14 count white Aida

Cross Stitch-2 strands

▽	3348	lt green
♣	3346	green
=	739	lt tan
S	738	tan
O	437	vy lt brown
✕	436	lt brown
♥	435	brown
→	434	dk brown
⊞	801	vy dk brown
I	310	black
·	blanc	white

Backstitch-1 strand

╱	3346	green
╱	310	black

French Knot-2 strands

●	310	black
●	blanc	white

Lazy Daisy Stitch-2 strands

⊘	209	lt purple

Chick

Stitch Count: 27w x 31h

Design Size: 2" x 2¼" on 14 count white Aida

Cross Stitch-2 strands

○	744	lt yellow
Y	743	lt yellow orange
☆	742	yellow orange
✳	3854	lt apricot
⊙	3853	apricot
⊞	470	green
■	310	black

Backstitch-1 strand

╱	310	black

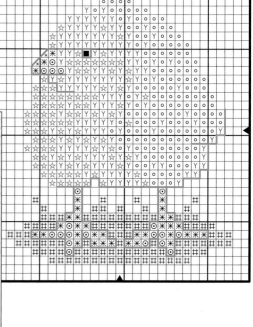

Rooster

Stitch Count: 33w x 34h

Design Size: 2⅜" x 2½" on 14 count white Aida

Cross Stitch-2 strands

=	3078	pale yellow
★	3822	pale gold
C	352	pale coral
✕	350	coral
▲	349	dk coral
∅	3827	lt brown
∿	976	brown
→	3826	dk brown
■	310	black
·	blanc	white

Backstitch-1 strand

╱	3826	dk brown
╱	310	black

French Knot -2 strands

○	blanc	white

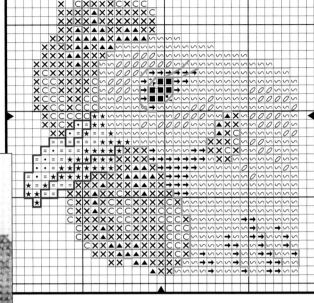

Dog

Stitch Count: 34w x 34h

Design Size: 2½" x 2½" on 14 count white Aida

Cross Stitch-2 strands

▫	754	lt peach
∧	3855	lt apricot
=	3827	vy lt golden brown
✳	977	lt golden brown
⊙	976	golden brown
✚	3826	dk golden brown
✿	975	vy dk golden brown
▼	413	dk grey
■	310	black
·	blanc	white

Backstitch-1 strand

╱	310	black

Backstitch-2 strands

╱	blanc	white

Couching Stitch-1 strand

╱	762	vy lt grey

Goat

Stitch Count: 35w x 34h

Design Size: 2½" x 2½" on 14 count white Aida

Cross Stitch-2 strands

Symbol	Code	Color
⁄	772	lt yellow green
¢	3347	yellow green
T	3345	dk yellow green
→	436	vy lt brown
m	435	lt brown
✕	434	brown
I	433	dk brown
●	801	vy dk brown
=	762	vy lt grey
◆	310	black
O	blanc	white

Backstitch-1 strand

⁄	310	black

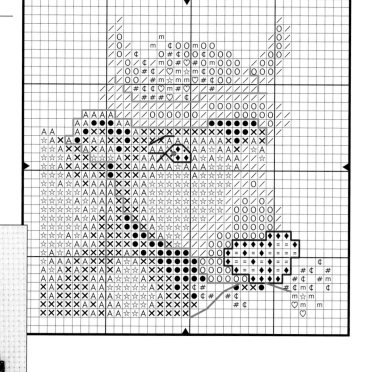

Cow

Stitch Count: 35w x 35h

Design Size: 2½" x 2½" on 14 count white Aida

Cross Stitch-2 strands

Symbol	Code	Color
m	666	lt red
♡	321	red
¢	368	lt green
#	367	green
⁄	712	cream
☆	977	lt golden brown
A	976	golden brown
✕	3826	dk golden brown
●	975	vy dk golden brown
=	413	dk grey
◆	310	black
O	3865	winter white

Backstitch-1 strand

⁄	367	green
⁄	975	vy dk golden brown
⁄	310	black

French Knot-2 strands

●	3865	winter white

Cat

Stitch Count: 34w x 31h

Design Size: 2½" x 2¼" on 14 count white Aida

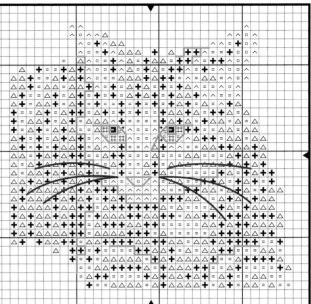

Cross Stitch-2 strands

▫	754	lt peach
⊞	470	green
^	644	lt beige grey
=	642	beige grey
△	646	grey
✚	645	dk grey
■	310	black

Backstitch-1 strand

╱	310	black

Backstitch-2 strands

╱	blanc	white

Couching Stitch-2 strands

╱	blanc	white

Sheep

Stitch Count: 35w x 34h

Design Size: 2½" x 2½" on 14 count white Aida

Cross Stitch-2 strands

◇	761	lt pink
=	955	lt mint green
∽	913	mint green
⌀	822	off white
#	644	beige grey
✕	642	dk beige grey
■	310	black
·	blanc	white

Backstitch-1 strand

╱	3328	pink
╱	909	dk mint green
╱	3781	vy dk beige grey
╱	310	black

French Knot-2 strands

●	blanc	white

Pig

Stitch Count: 35w x 35h

Design Size: 2½" x 2½" on 14 count white Aida

Cross Stitch-2 strands

⊘	963	lt pink
♡	3716	pink
#	368	lt green
A	320	green
+	3840	blue
O	3838	dk blue
=	762	pale grey
C	415	lt grey
✖	318	grey
◆	414	dk grey
●	310	black
▫	blanc	white

Backstitch-1 strand

╱	310	black
╱	963	lt pink
╱	320	green
╱	3838	dk blue

French Knot-2 strands

●	blanc	white

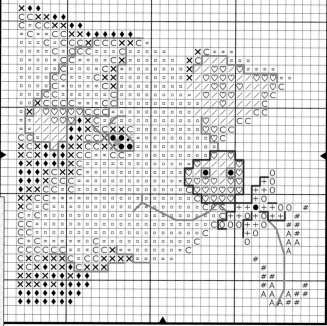

Bunny

Stitch Count: 27w x 30h

Design Size: 2" x 2¼" on 14 count white Aida

Cross Stitch-2 strands

♡	963	lt pink
+	962	pink
╱	745	lt yellow
☆	743	lt yellow orange
#	741	orange
A	470	green
=	739	lt tan
✖	436	lt brown
●	433	brown
◆	648	lt grey
O	blanc	white

Backstitch-1 strand

╱	3799	charcoal

French Knot-2 strands

●	blanc	white

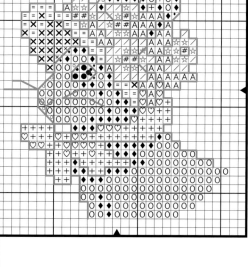

Forest Animals

Celebrate the serenity of the forest with enchanting portraits of its wildlife, from the owl and squirrel to bears and a fox. You'll also spot a wolf, a doe, a raccoon, a chipmunk, and a moose.

Squirrel

Stitch Count: 32w x 34h

Design Size: 2⅜" x 2½" on 14 count white Aida

Cross Stitch-2 strands

✳	977	lt golden brown
✖	435	lt brown
^	644	lt beige-grey
=	642	beige-grey
△	646	dusty grey
✚	645	dk dusty grey
~	762	vy lt grey
Y	415	lt grey
■	310	black
•	blanc	white

Backstitch-1 strand

╱	310	black

Backstitch-2 strands

╱	blanc	white

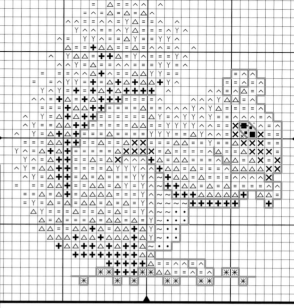

Wolf

Stitch Count: 32w x 33h

Design Size: 2⅜" x 2⅜" on 14 count white Aida

Cross Stitch-2 strands

✖	435	lt brown
~	762	vy lt grey
⊙	318	grey
^	644	lt beige-grey
◇	642	beige-grey
⊠	645	dusty grey
▼	844	dk dusty grey
■	310	black
•	blanc	white

Backstitch-1 strand

╱	310	black

French Knot-2 strands

○	blanc	white

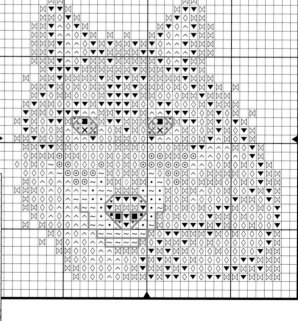

Fox

Stitch Count: 31w x 33h

Design Size: 2¼" x 2⅜" on 14 count white Aida

Cross Stitch-2 strands

Y	3854	lt apricot
+	3853	apricot
✳	921	rust
✿	920	dk rust
◆	433	brown
=	415	lt grey
■	317	grey
▼	3799	charcoal
•	blanc	white

Backstitch-1 strand

╱	310	black

Backstitch-2 strands

╱	blanc	white

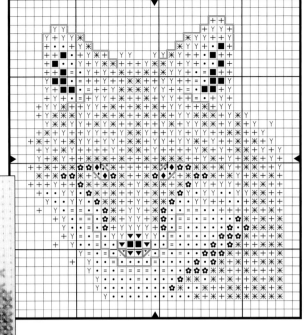

Doe

Stitch Count: 30w x 31h

Design Size: 2¼" x 2¼" on 14 count white Aida

Cross Stitch-2 strands

∧	739	lt tan
☆	437	lt brown
✳	435	brown
⧋	975	golden brown
~	762	vy lt grey
=	415	lt grey
▼	3799	charcoal
■	310	black
•	blanc	white

Backstitch-1 strand

╱	310	black

Backstitch-2 strands

╱	blanc	white

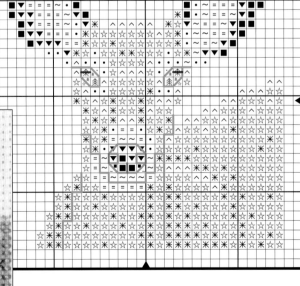

Raccoon

Stitch Count: 35w x 29h

Design Size: 2½" x 2⅛" on 14 count white Aida

Cross Stitch-2 strands

╱	762	pale grey
+	415	vy lt grey
=	318	lt grey
☆	414	grey
C	317	dk grey
✕	413	vy dk grey
◆	3799	charcoal
●	310	black

Backstitch-1 strand

╱	310	black
╱	blanc	white

French Knot-2 strands

●	blanc	white

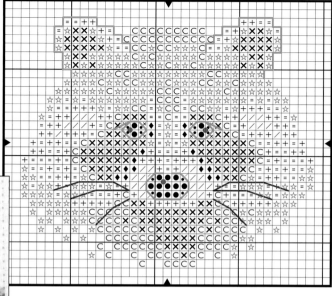

Bear

Stitch Count: 34w x 31h

Design Size: 2½" x 2¼" on 14 count white Aida

Cross Stitch-2 strands

⊡	712	cream
⊘	739	lt tan
◇	738	tan
=	437	dk tan
∽	436	vy dk tan
C	435	vy lt brown
#	434	lt brown
✕	433	brown
▲	801	dk brown
■	310	black

Backstitch-1 strand

╱	310	black
╱	938	vy dk brown

French Knot-2 strands

●	712	cream

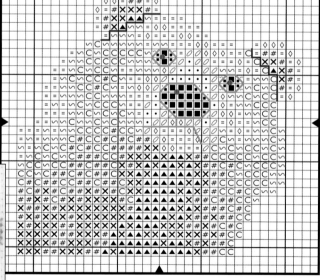

Chipmunk

Stitch Count: 35w x 35h

Design Size: 2½" x 2½" on 14 count white Aida

Cross Stitch-2 strands

△	3348	lt green
m	3347	green
◒	3346	dk green
➡	712	cream
★	739	lt tan
⅏	436	vy lt brown
2	435	lt brown
♥	434	brown
枾	433	dk brown
▨	938	vy dk brown
■	310	black
O	blanc	white

Backstitch-1 strand

/	938	vy dk brown
/	310	black

French Knot-2 strands

●	blanc	white

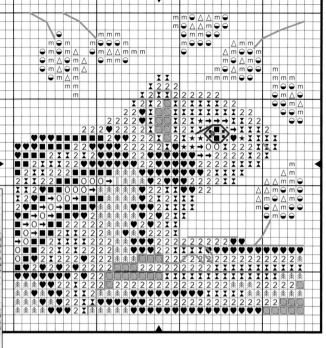

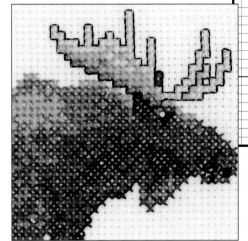

Moose

Stitch Count: 33w x 33h

Design Size: 2⅜" x 2⅜" on 14 count white Aida

Cross Stitch-2 strands

∧	739	lt tan
◇	437	pale brown
✳	435	lt brown
◆	433	brown
●	938	dk brown
▼	844	dk grey
■	310	black

Backstitch-1 strand

/	310	black

French Knot-2 strands

○	blanc	white

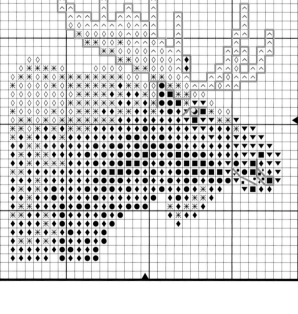

Owl

Stitch Count: 33w x 31h

Design Size: 2⅜" x 2¼" on 14 count white Aida

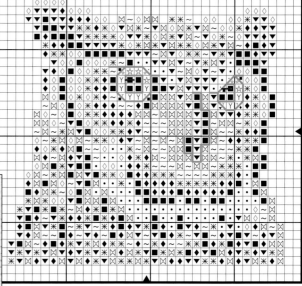

Cross Stitch-2 strands

Y	743	lt yellow orange
☆	742	yellow orange
◇	437	pale brown
✳	435	lt brown
◆	433	brown
~	762	pale grey
⊠	318	lt grey
▼	413	dk grey
■	310	black
·	blanc	white

Backstitch-1 strand

╱	310	black

Backstitch-2 strands

╱	blanc	white

Black Bear

Stitch Count: 35w x 35h

Design Size: 2½" x 2½" on 14 count white Aida

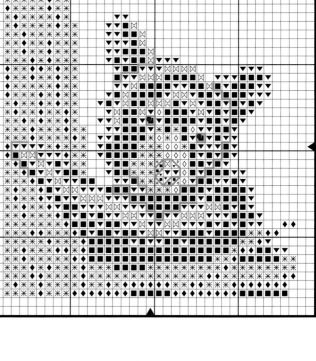

Cross Stitch-2 strands

◇	437	pale brown
✳	435	lt brown
◆	433	brown
⊠	646	grey
▼	844	dk grey
■	310	black

Backstitch-1 strand

╱	310	black

French Knot-2 strands

•	blanc	white

Ocean Animals

The ocean is alive with a wide array of creatures, from the tiny seahorse to the giant whale. Delve into the deep to find colorful fish, an octopus, dolphin, porpoise, shark, sea turtle, and crab.

Blue Tang

Stitch Count: 35w x 35h

Design Size: 2½" x 2½" on 14 count white Aida

Cross Stitch-2 strands

Y	743	yellow
⊙	519	sky blue
+	996	lt bright blue
◆	995	bright blue
^	472	lt green
⊙	470	green
C	415	lt grey
■	310	black

Cross Stitch-1 strand

⊞	813	blue

Backstitch-1 strand

/	310	black

French Knot-2 strands

●	blanc	white

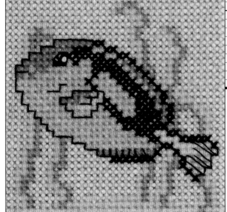

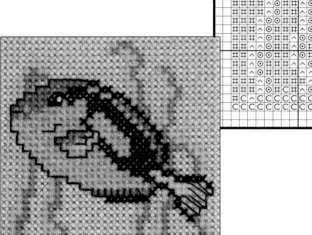

Dolphin

Stitch Count: 28w x 28h

Design Size: 2" x 2" on 14 count white Aida

Cross Stitch-2 strands

+	605	lt pink
♡	604	pink
╱	800	lt blue
☆	794	blue
╥	799	dk blue
=	762	pale grey
A	415	vy lt grey
#	318	lt grey
✕	414	grey
●	3799	charcoal
◆	310	black
O	blanc	white

Backstitch-1 strand

/	3799	charcoal
/	310	black

French Knot-2 strands

●	blanc	white

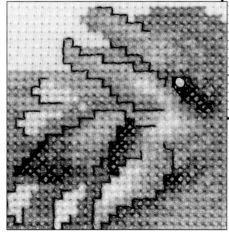

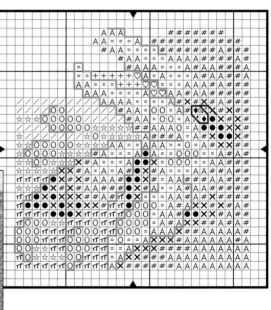

Porpoise

Stitch Count: 35w x 29h

Design Size: 2½" x 2⅛" on 14 count white Aida

Cross Stitch-2 strands

=	827	lt blue
⊞	813	blue
+	826	dk blue
~	762	vy lt grey
♥	415	lt grey
⊠	318	dk grey
⊡	414	grey
■	310	black
•	blanc	white

Backstitch-1 strand

/	310	black

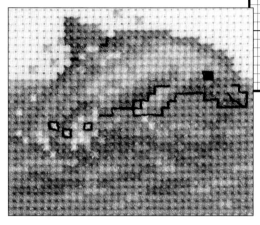

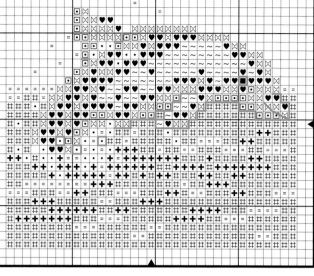

Clownfish

Stitch Count: 35w x 35h

Design Size: 2½" x 2½" on 14 count white Aida

Cross Stitch-2 strands

◇	740	bright orange
+	721	orange
△	720	dk orange
^	472	lt green
⊙	470	green
Y	415	grey
■	310	black
•	blanc	white

Cross Stitch-1 strand

⊞	813	blue

Backstitch-1 strand

/	310	black

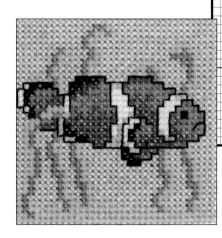

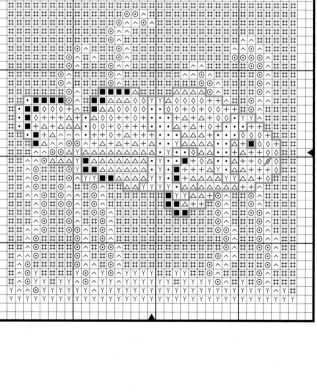

Seahorse

Stitch Count: 28w x 28h

Design Size: 2" x 2" on 14 count white Aida

Cross Stitch-2 strands

𝍤	604	pink
J	744	lt yellow
O	742	yellow
X	722	lt orange
◢	721	orange
♣	704	green
∿	798	blue
¢	340	lt purple
▯	310	black
▫	blanc	white

Backstitch-1 strand

/	433	brown
/	310	black

French Knot-2 strands

○	blanc	white

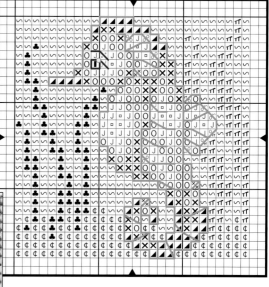

Crab

Stitch Count: 35w x 35h

Design Size: 2½" x 2½" on 14 count white Aida

Cross Stitch-2 strands

▫	948	pale peach
=	353	vy pale coral
⊞	352	pale coral
◇	813	lt blue
+	826	blue
⊙	642	beige grey
◆	645	dk grey
■	310	black
·	blanc	white

Backstitch-1 strand

/	310	black

French Knot-2 strands

●	blanc	white

Sea Turtle

Stitch Count: 35w x 35h

Design Size: 2½" x 2½" on 14 count white Aida

Cross Stitch-2 strands

Y	743	yellow-orange
^	3855	apricot
♡	3827	lt golden brown
⊙	976	golden brown
✛	3826	dk golden brown
●	975	vy dk golden brown
■	310	black

Cross Stitch-1 strand

=	827	lt blue
⊞	813	blue
➡	826	dk blue

Backstitch-1 strand

╱	310	black

Backstitch-2 strands

╱	3855	apricot

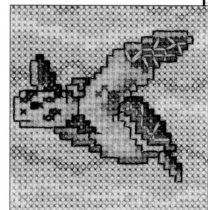

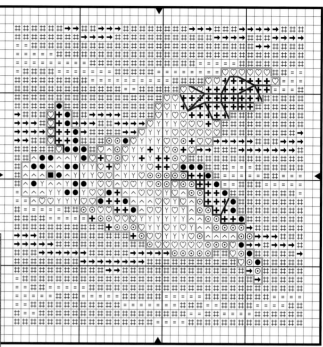

Shark

Stitch Count: 35w x 35h

Design Size: 2½" x 2½" on 14 count white Aida

Cross Stitch-2 strands

~	762	vy lt grey
♡	415	lt grey
⊠	318	grey
⊡	414	dk grey
3	317	vy dk grey
■	310	black
•	blanc	white

Cross Stitch-1 strand

=	827	lt blue
⊞	813	blue
✛	826	dk blue

Backstitch-1 strand

╱	310	black

Backstitch-2 strands

╱	blanc	white

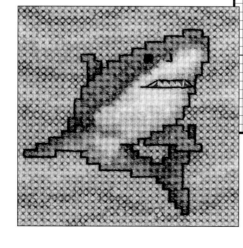

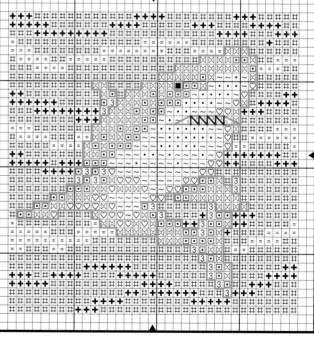

Octopus

Stitch Count: 35w x 35h

Design Size: 2½" x 2½" on 14 count white Aida

Cross Stitch-2 strands

□	948	lt peach
~	945	tawny
=	353	lt coral
⊞	352	coral
✚	351	dk coral
■	310	black
·	blanc	white

Cross Stitch-1 strand

◇	827	lt blue
⊙	813	blue
◆	826	dk blue

Backstitch-1 strand

╱	310	black

Backstitch-2 strands

╱	blanc	white

French Knot-2 strands

○	blanc	white

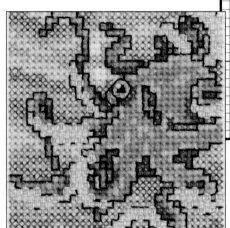

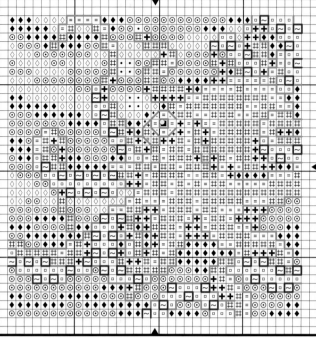

Whale Tail

Stitch Count: 35w x 34h

Design Size: 2½" x 2½" on 14 count white Aida

Cross Stitch-2 strands

=	827	pale blue
⊞	813	lt blue
✚	826	blue
~	762	vy pale grey
Y	415	pale grey
▼	3799	charcoal
■	310	black
·	blanc	white

Backstitch-1 strand

╱	310	black

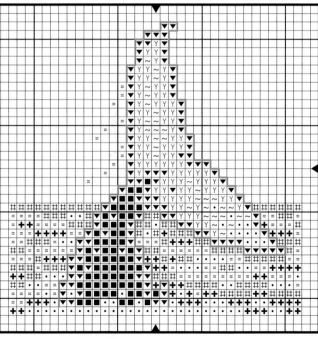

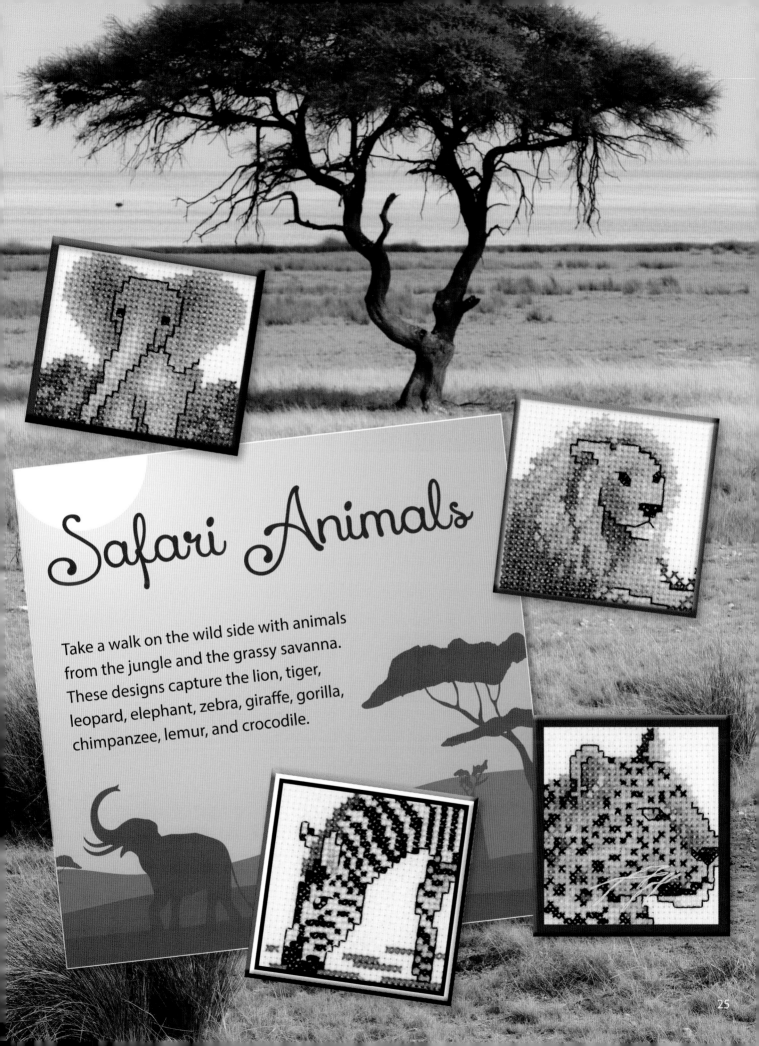

Safari Animals

Take a walk on the wild side with animals from the jungle and the grassy savanna. These designs capture the lion, tiger, leopard, elephant, zebra, giraffe, gorilla, chimpanzee, lemur, and crocodile.

Chimp

Stitch Count: 35w x 32h

Design Size: 2½" x 2⅜" on 14 count white Aida

Cross Stitch-2 strands

3	948	lt peach
⁄	754	peach
▨	353	lt coral
→	317	grey
2	413	dk grey
♥	3799	charcoal
■	310	black
O	blanc	white

Backstitch-1 strand

⁄	310	black

French Knot-2 strands

●	blanc	white

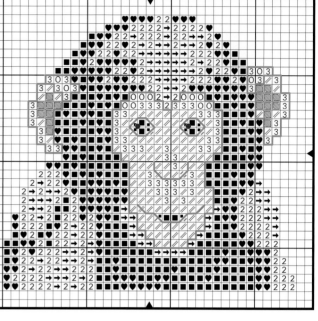

Lion

Stitch Count: 35w x 33h

Design Size: 2½" x 2⅜" on 14 count white Aida

Cross Stitch-2 strands

⋒	3822	vy lt antique gold
★	3821	lt antique gold
⁄	3820	antique gold
ⲭ	783	gold
m	782	dk gold
→	780	vy dk gold
4	469	olive green
■	936	dk olive green
2	762	vy lt grey
♥	415	lt grey
●	310	black
O	blanc	white

Backstitch-1 strand

⁄	310	black

Zebra

Stitch Count: 35w x 35h

Design Size: 2½" x 2½" on 14 count white Aida

Cross Stitch-2 strands

4	3346	green
2	435	lt brown
♥	434	brown
Ⅺ	762	vy lt grey
⁄	415	lt grey
▨	318	grey
■	310	black
O	blanc	white

Backstitch-1 strand

⁄	310	black

French Knot-2 strands

●	blanc	white

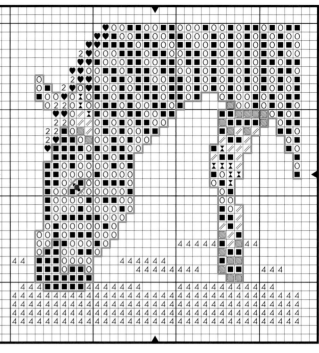

Tiger

Stitch Count: 35w x 35h

Design Size: 2½" x 2½" on 14 count white Aida

Cross Stitch-2 strands

▲	353	vy lt coral
m	3348	lt green
◖	3346	green
→	3822	lt antique gold
2	3821	antique gold
Ⅺ	3820	dk antique gold
★	783	gold
▨	782	dk gold
⁄	762	lt grey
♥	415	grey
■	310	black
O	blanc	white

Backstitch-1 strand

⁄	310	black

Lemur

Stitch Count: 35w x 32h

Design Size: 2½" x 2⅜" on 14 count white Aida

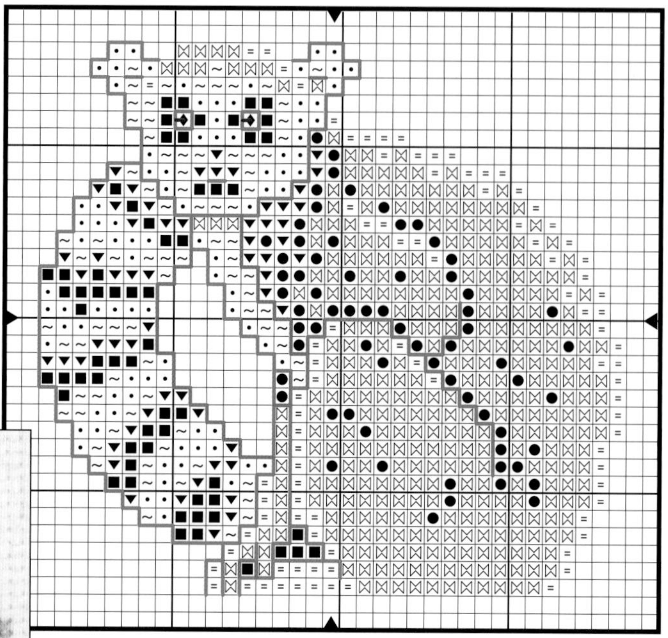

Cross Stitch-2 strands

♦	433	brown
~	762	vy lt grey
=	415	lt grey
⊠	318	grey
●	317	dk grey
▼	3799	charcoal
■	310	black
•	blanc	white

Backstitch-1 strand

/	310	black

Backstitch-2 strands

/	blanc	white

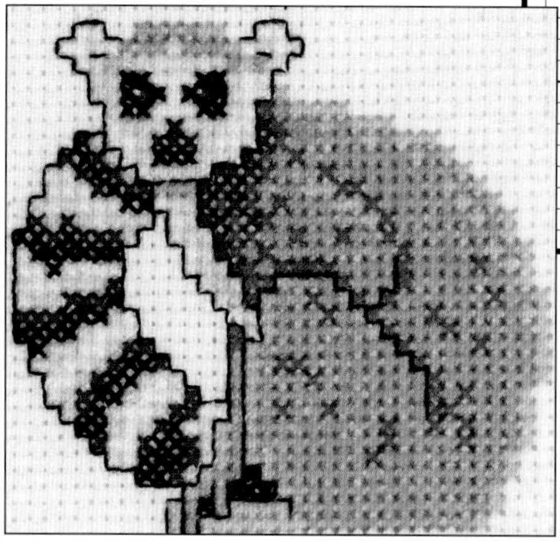

Crocodile

Stitch Count: 35w x 34h

Design Size: 2½" x 2½" on 14 count white Aida

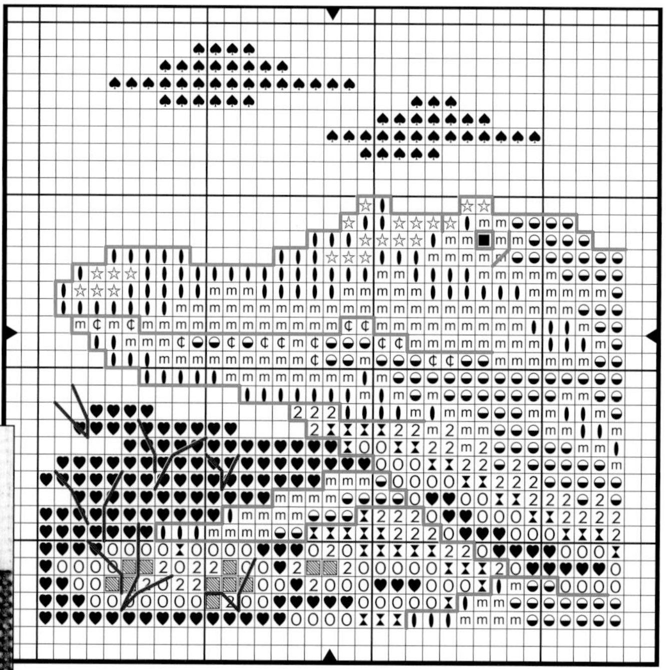

Cross Stitch-2 strands

♠	3756	vy lt blue
♥	712	cream
O	739	lt tan
⧗	738	tan
2	437	vy lt brown
▨	436	lt brown
☆	613	lt drab brown
⬮	612	drab brown
m	611	dk drab brown
◒	610	vy dk drab brown
■	310	black
¢	blanc	white

Backstitch-1 strand

/	310	black
/	610	vy dk drab brown

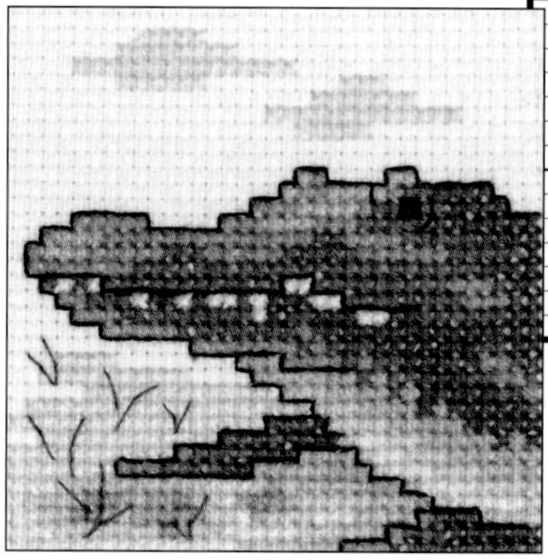

Elephant

Stitch Count: 35w x 30h

Design Size: 2½" x 2¼" on 14 count white Aida

Cross Stitch-2 strands

·	3072	vy lt grey green
◊	3347	green
▲	3345	dk green
⊘	648	lt grey
C	647	grey
#	646	dk grey
✕	645	vy dk grey
●	310	black

Backstitch-1 strand

╱	310	black

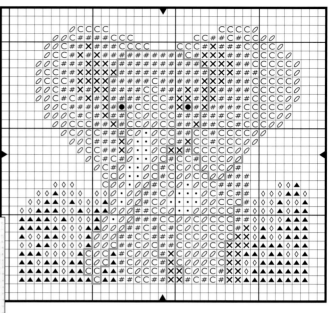

Giraffe

Stitch Count: 35w x 33h

Design Size: 2½" x 2⅜" on 14 count white Aida

Cross Stitch-2 strands

=	3347	green
✕	3345	dk green
→	739	vy lt tan
O	738	lt tan
♥	437	tan
3	436	dk tan
⊠	435	lt brown
╱	434	brown
▨	433	dk brown
■	310	black

Backstitch-1 strand

╱	310	black

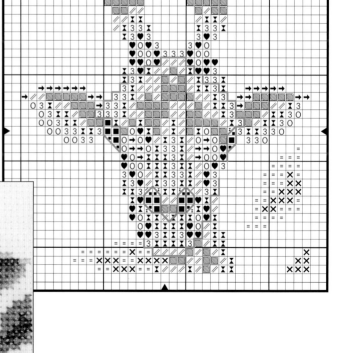

Leopard

Stitch Count: 32w x 35h

Design Size: 2⅜" x 2½" on 14 count white Aida

Cross Stitch-2 strands

∧	3855	pale apricot
=	3827	vy lt golden brown
✳	977	lt golden brown
⊙	976	golden brown
✚	3826	dk golden brown
●	975	vy dk golden brown
~	762	pale grey
▼	3799	charcoal
■	310	black
·	blanc	white

Backstitch-1 strand

╱	310	black

Backstitch-2 strands

╱	310	black
╱	blanc	white

Couching Stitch-2 strands

╱	blanc	white

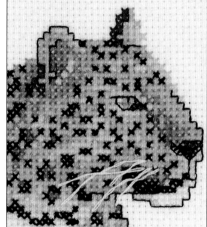

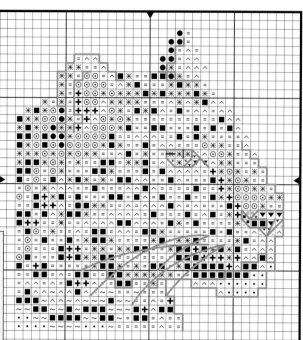

Gorilla

Stitch Count: 35w x 33h

Design Size: 2½" x 2⅜" on 14 count white Aida

Cross Stitch-2 strands

♡	772	vy lt green
★	3348	lt green
m	3347	green
▨	3346	dk green
0	762	pale grey
→	415	vy lt grey
4	318	lt grey
♥	414	grey
╱	317	dk grey
✗	413	vy dk grey
2	3799	charcoal
■	310	black

Backstitch-1 strand

╱	310	black

General Instructions

HOW TO READ CHARTS

Each chart is made up of a key and a gridded design on which each square represents a stitch. The symbols in the key tell which floss color to use for each stitch on the chart. The key will indicate the stitch and how many strands to use.

 A square filled with a full-size symbol should be worked as a **Cross Stitch**.

 A reduced symbol in a corner of the square is usually worked as a **One-Quarter Stitch**. A reduced symbol in a corner of the square should be worked as a **Three-Quarter Stitch** when a Backstitch crosses two squares.

Three-Quarter Stitch

No Stitch

 A straight line should be worked as a **Backstitch** or **Couching Stitch**. The color key will indicate which stitch to work.

 A large dot should be worked as a **French Knot**.

 An oval should be worked as a **Lazy Daisy Stitch**.

Sometimes the symbol for a Cross Stitch will be partially covered when a Backstitch, Couching Stitch, French Knot, or Lazy Daisy Stitch crosses that square.

GETTING STARTED

Preparing Fabric

Cut your fabric at least 3" larger on all sides and overcast the edges. It is better to waste a little fabric than to come up short after many hours of stitching.

Working with Floss

To ensure smoother stitches, separate strands and realign them before threading the needle. Keep stitching tension consistent. Begin and end floss by running under several stitches on the back; do not tie knots.

Where to Start

The horizontal and vertical centers of each charted design are shown by arrows. You may start at any point on the charted design, but be sure the design will be centered on the fabric. Locate the center of the fabric by folding it in half, top to bottom and again left to right. On the charted design, count the number of squares (stitches) from the center of the chart to where you wish to start. Then, from the fabric's center, find your starting point by counting out the same number of fabric threads (stitches).

HOW TO STITCH

Always work Cross Stitches, One-Quarter Stitches, and Three-Quarter Stitches first; then add the Backstitch, Couching Stitch, French Knots, and Lazy Daisy Stitches. When stitching, bring the threaded needle up at 1 and all odd numbers and down at 2 and all even numbers.

Cross Stitch: For horizontal rows, work stitches in two journeys *(Fig. 1)*. For vertical rows, complete each stitch as shown *(Fig. 2)*.

Fig. 1

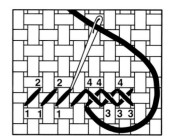

Fig. 2

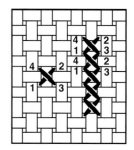

One-Quarter Stitch and **Three-Quarter Stitch:** Stitch 1-2 is the One-Quarter Stitch *(Fig. 3)*. When stitches 1-4 are worked in the same color, the resulting stitch is called a Three-Quarter Stitch.

Fig. 3

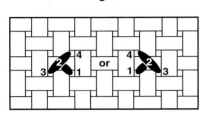

Backstitch: For outlines and details, Backstitch should be worked after the design has been completed *(Fig. 4)*.

Fig. 4

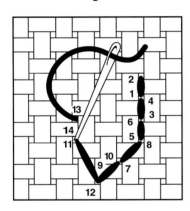

Couching Stitch: For details, Couching Stitches should be worked after the design has been completed. Bring needle up through fabric at one end of line; insert needle at opposite end of line, gently shaping floss to mimic line on chart. With another needle threaded with matching color floss, use very small stitches to tack the first floss strand to the design *(Fig. 5)*. Secure all floss ends on the wrong side and clip the floss ends.

Fig. 5

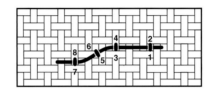

Straight Stitch: Bring the needle up at 1; go down at 2 *(Fig. 6)*.

Fig. 6

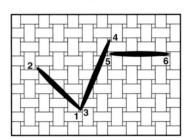

French Knot: Bring the needle up at 1. Wrap the floss twice around the needle. Insert the needle at 2, tighten the knot, and pull the needle through the fabric, holding the floss until it must be released *(Fig. 7)*.

Fig. 7

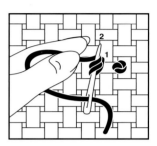

Lazy Daisy Stitch: Bring the needle up at 1 and make a loop. Go down at 1 and come up at 2, keeping the floss below the point of the needle *(Fig. 8)*. Pull the needle through and go down at 3 to anchor the loop, completing the stitch.

Fig. 8

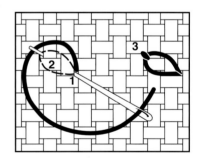

Production Team: Technical Writer – Mary Sullivan Hutcheson; Technical Associate – Jean Lewis; Editorial Writer – Susan Frantz Wiles; Senior Graphic Artist – Lora Puls; Graphic Artist – Kellie McAnulty; Contributing Graphic Artist – C. Waynette Traub.